Around the Bend

poems by

Colleen Wells

Finishing Line Press
Georgetown, Kentucky

Around the Bend

For Susan—with whom many struggles have been shared.

*"The secret of change is to focus all of your energy
not on fighting the old, but on building the new."*
—Socrates

ACKNOWLEDGMENTS

"Once Every Seventeen Years" was published in *Ryder*
"Reframing," "The Serpent with Two Tales," and "A Dose of Today" were
included in *SCARS: Poems & Short Stories About Mental Health and Healing*

Publisher: Leah Huete de Maines
Editor: Christen Kincaid
Cover Art: Janet Hitzeman Lynch
Author Photo: Becky Meek Photography
Cover Design: Elizabeth Maines McCleavy

Order online: www.finishinglinepress.com
also available on amazon.com

Author inquiries and mail orders:
Finishing Line Press
PO Box 1626
Georgetown, Kentucky 40324
USA

Contents

A Hallmark Moment

It is almost closing time,
and I can't find the right birthday card
when in walks a portly, disheveled,
woman with straw-like hair
that might have been more like silk
when she was a child,
or perhaps when she just washed it.

She surfs through the cards, giggles, and guffaws.
Next, the customer cruises the clearance aisle, her chortles
turning to chokes.
Then she starts spinning through the ornaments
while howling with laughter.

That's when the woman approaches me
and says,
"Thank you."

I can smell liquor
on her breath.
Broken capillaries squiggle
across red cheeks.
The gleam in her eyes
tells me something
besides alcohol and Hallmark humor
tickles her brain.

When I'm done shopping, I walk down toward the restaurants
and see a group of people at the tables
outside a deli,
shopping carts, and trash bags piled around them.

The woman from the store is there, too.
She seems to be holding court,
a queen amongst her jesters.

Take a few things away—
Aveda shampoo, an expensive shrink, health insurance,
and I might be seated there, too.

A Party of Five Becomes Two

I miss the thump of their footsteps on stairs-
each of them different, like songs sung
from the soles of their feet.

I would now welcome his belch at the dinner table,
little sister protesting,
a new rule emerging,
"One and done!"

I know who was most likely
to use the last of the shredded cheddar,
an irritant I'd embrace today.

Siblings fighting over the remote control,
or whose turn to do dishes,
garnering them the nicknames of
"Frick and Frack."

Mostly I crave the sound
of their laughter,
belly-full,
the echoes of sunshine.

And dancing in the kitchen
feet thunking against tile,
hands pumping in the air,
clapping a rhythm so sweet,
it hurts.

Hello, Walls

Depression has eked its way in again.
I've tried reiki, self-help books, walking,
engaging my spiritual guides,
and good old-fashioned prayer.

I try to simply choose happy, but happy doesn't choose me.
I live with bipolar disorder, and
a doctor once told me they think
depression is harder on the brain than mania.
What's the matter with my grey matter?

I wish I never had this mood disorder.
I try not to whine too much about it.
I just keep going,
but this time, I'm running into
 walls.

Sputtering Again

Here I am, home from work.
Being around my coworkers
boosted my spirit.

So why was it so hard to go in?
Now at home,
I'm sad, overwhelmed,
wondering what to do next.

This is a vicious cycle.
I wonder when it will end,
but for now,
I sputter like a car on empty,
choking for fuel.

Start with the Laundry

Today, I awoke, swallowed
by despair.
I started making a list.
The more I added to it,
the more I thought I'd never get it all done.

And the darkness grew,
threatening to undo me.
So, I started with the laundry.

Now it's six and a half hours later.
There's still plenty to do,
yet plenty has been done, too.
And I'm still here,
not blooming exactly,
  but rooted.

Heartblast

I was in Hobby Lobby by myself
ho-hum looking for tags
and decided to get
some Valentine's Day napkins for a bit of cheer.

I spied boxes of Valentine's cards for children,
felt a shockwave in my heart
recalling how selective Gaelle was
in choosing those
for her classmates.

It was a pain,
and now, I'm remembering
how often we'd come to this store,
looking for a craft to do,
cruising the clearance,
searching for wall art for her room
—always pink and glittery!

How I miss those days,
even the fussiness of it,
and there among the Valentine's Day cards,
my heart cracked wide open.

Babies and Brains

Feeling a bit raw,
had my assessment today
with the replacement
for my psychiatrist,
whom I'd worked with for over ten years.

I trusted her so much.
This new person is a nurse practitioner
who tells me she worked for seventeen years
as a nurse delivering babies before moving into psychiatry.

Babies and brains,
  is there anything more fragile?
This alone,
  planted a seed of new trust.

Love it or List it

Love it or list it?

At first, I balked at the
huge task of emptying out
from the past ten years
of raising kids here,
and a passel of pets,
some who have died,
and others still along for the ride.

Empty nest is not for the faint of heart.
At times the rawness of it overwhelms me,
but I'm finally in a place where I'm able to start this next step.

Knowing I will miss the voluminous screened porch
where I've spent endless hours painting furniture,
the large kitchen island where I put out food for my family,
the bay window in our dining room overflowing with succulents,
the tread of stairs that housed the sound of our kids coming and
     going,
and our pillared front porch where Rick and I watched for
     hummingbirds.

I think I will even miss our scroungy basement
now rife with possibilities of the next owner finishing it,
but I'm ready for new beginnings somewhere else.

I'm ready to love it, and I'm ready to list it.

What it is

Sadness is the saggy gray sweatpants with the faint orange stain on the leg that you wear anyway. It is the shrill cry of the black dog frightened out of its mind by the racket of the shelter.

It is also seeing the calendar flip to June and there's nothing to show for it. No goals accomplished. No savings in the bank. Sadness takes many forms.

Sadness comes and sadness goes, but it seems to want to stay. It's the small chip in the teacup you know is there, but that others likely do not see.

It's the despair hanging in the milky eyes of the elderly who've lost everything but must get up again to face another day. It's the fast car and the squirrel that didn't get away.

Sadness seems like something I'd never make time for, but it's taking all of my time.

Snow Day

Out the window during my lunch break,
a confetti snowfall
blankets the lawn, cars, driveway, and trees.
My boss just texted they're leaving early.
I don't have to come back in.
A snow day! A victory!

Then a slam to my solar plexus,
I think of the kids whooping and hollering
clapping and slapping
in the moments school got called off for snow.

Take me back to those days, I lament,
as the ghosts continue to shout,
"No school! No school!"

Small Meals and Scrabble

Rick and I are getting used to the routine of two,
small meals and Scrabble.
When the kids do converge,
raiding the fridge,
making a ruckus,
disrupting the day of whatever is planned,

admittedly, it's the quiet I crave.

The Wisdom of Forty-five

I'm fifty and work an entry-level job
doing activities with seniors.
Due to Covid-19, we've been unable
to be with residents.

The activities staff are doing things for
other departments to fill our days,
and it has given me time
to fill my head with negative chatter:

I'm fifty. I work an entry-level job.
I don't make enough money.
I'm a loser, and so on.

And then I think about
what my boss once said. She's forty-five.
She said thinking about the residents
alone in their rooms
day in and day out,
should make anyone unable to feel sorry for themselves.

And she's so right.

Marching Orders

I can't believe it's almost March,
that we're this far into the new year.
Why does life have to speed up
as we age?

A sense of losing months
makes sadness even more sinister.
Days wasted in doldrums;
depression is a tricky thief.

March, hello,
  do you hear me?
This must stop!
Those are your marching orders.

Reframing

The bare limbs of the birch tree
jut out, naked,
no signs of spring
and the bee balm
looks stringy and tired,
against a backdrop of sludgy snow.

The window framing my view
is dirty, and the plants along the ledge slouch
under winter's breath heaving in through the old panes of glass.

Maybe I should have gone to work after all,
or maybe I'm best at home.
Either way,
I've got to reframe my view.

Walking on Sunshine

The sun peaked out yesterday,
and the high was forty-three,
the likes of which we haven't
seen in a good month.

So, I went out for a brief walk;
I wasn't exactly walking on sunshine,
but at least I was walking in it.

Random Page not so Random

Sometimes I open inspirational books at random to see if
there's an answer in them for whatever is bothering me.
Today what's festering is I just
want to be a writer and work on my furniture side hustle.
I don't want to work at anything else.
And yet,
my job is helping with activities for the elderly.

So, I opened a book by Jim Henson.
It said on page 99,
"Wake up in the morning
get yourself to work.
Fraggles never fool around.
Fraggles never shirk.
Your duty's always waiting
and duty must be done.
There's ping-pong games that must be played
and songs that must be sung."
—Gobo and the Fraggles

It's Not Easy Being Green—and Other Things to Consider
by Jim Henson

The Serpent with two Tales

Depression.
You will it away, but you're well-versed in sadness—
enough to know it doesn't work like that.

Go to bed early, wake up late.
It can't find you in your sleep,
except for that one night
you dreamed of a serpent with two tails.

Try to remember what it felt like to laugh,
and realize the memory is like distant thunder.
Way. Way. In the distance.

When is the last time you danced in the kitchen,
or looked in the mirror and saw something pretty?
Where is the writer's high when time disappears
along with your cares?

Gone is the will to get excited over a call from a good friend,
the desire for anything specific to eat,
except the coffee that keeps you going.

Drum up ways you could go,
pills and you can drift off to sleep,
except you might only take enough to damage
your brain, not shut it down.

Eye the door. Remember the scene in the movie
with the door and the belt.
But would what worked for her, work for you too?
It was just a movie.

No option is optimal because you know deep down
you don't really want to die.
You just want it to stop.

Surprise!

A big surprise about the day our daughter went away to college was
I didn't cry as much as I thought I would.
A bigger surprise is not a day goes by that I don't miss her,
and wish she could come home.

Every day,
the same surprise.

I'd rather get flowers.

Checklist

Took my mood stabilizer—check!
Took my vitamin D supplement—check!
Showered—check!
Went for a walk in the sun—check!
Crossed off my list of chores—check!
Ate a salad for lunch—check!

Still depressed—check!

Ship of Fools

I have a roof over my head,
  food in the fridge.
Right there, is more than most in the world.

Freedom to come and go as I please,
  and it's a sunny day.
So why do I feel so low?

Neurotransmitters not firing?
Low serotonin levels?
The lack of estrogen?

Can I ever right this ship,
or am I forever going to
sail on a ship of fools?

To Fill

My psychiatric nurse practitioner
agreed to tinker with my meds.
I told her how hard I've been trying, but I still feel
a lack of joy and disinterest in many of
the things that used to bring me happiness.
I'm sleeping nine or ten hours a night too,
even though winter has passed.

We agree to add back in the anti-depressant
I was taken off of a year ago when I had mania.
I've never been this excited
to take a medication in my life.

A text tells me it's been filled at the pharmacy already.
I pray it will fill up
the emptiness.

Vernal Equinox

It's March 20th,
spring has sprung,
and just in time.

The sunny days
and breezy air,
daffodils bobbing in it all.

Things are greener.
A landscape
painting me back to life.

March Madness

Going through old journals and pictures as I clean,
reminds me how much time has passed.
Outside, the wind creaks through the trees
swaying branches as memories waft
through my brain
like the dust kicked up and stirred
from shaking the tablecloth out.

I'm a half-century old,
a little bit wiser,
a bit more reserved,
and suddenly wracked with grief
by these photographs of happier days.

The perils of spring cleaning.

The Flea

An endless sea of
stuff to pack
engulfs me,
pulls me into a swell of anxiety.
I pick away at it,
flitting from one pile
to the next,
like I'm at a flea market,
which is actually
where a lot of this stuff came from.

The Gambler

Our frail, elderly Jack Russell
is one day closer to going to heaven.
He has a host of health issues,
 and now has stopped eating.

He will probably be euthanized tomorrow.

Kramer spends most of his time
swaddled up in a blanket
next to my husband.

His little head rests on the edge of the couch.
He peers over at me.
I study his brown eyes,
not seeing pain, hunger, or even resignation.

He holds his cards close to his chest
but the hollowing sockets
that hold those eyes
tell another story.

A Dose of Today

Take your medicine, the 150 mg of Bupropion
and 5 mg of Aripiprazole.
Take your vitamin D.

Wash it down with cold water or orange juice.
Grab some coffee on the way out.
Wait for the alchemy to begin.

Grow your to-do list,
write it down in blue,
start on it.

Feel bored, get tired, wonder what it's all for.
You're wading in the muck now.
Let it pull you down into sleep.

Wake up at four-thirty.
Get back to doing.
Check the list again.

Only five things are checked off.
Make some coffee, take a walk.
The sun is out now.
This is as good as it gets
  for today.

If There were Never Winter

If there were never winter,
then there'd never be spring.
Dogwoods popping and warm sunshine,
the sound of children playing
outside shushing the hush of winter.

The warm, nutty scent of coffee
perking in the pot
or pink lemonade
tarting the tip of my tongue,
the glass sweating in my hand.

The comfort of hiding
under layers of blankets on a cold night
or kicking them off
on a steaming July afternoon,
too hot even to nap.

The smell of chili bubbling
in the crockpot in October
or chicken and baked potatoes on the grill in June?
Boots and sweaters and crisp autumn air,
or bathing suits and trips to the beach?

Shimmering snow and children
rushing in for hot chocolate
after sledding
or bursting in for popsicles
after splashing in the pool?

You can't have morning without night,
winter without fall,
fall without summer,
and so on,
but,

just so you know, I'm writing this in April.
It's 73 degrees and sunny,
the birds are atwitter, chirping away.
Somewhere a mower's humming,
and oh, the blue sky.

Full Circle

From the porch, I watched the rain
form a puddle in the driveway;
perfect circles gathered within its borders,
each created by a quiet droplet.

How long had it been
since I watched
a gift like this?
Too long.

I marveled at the pattern.
It reminded me of some artwork
I'd done as a kid
of circles, painted in thick globs of red and yellow.
These water circles were as clear as a glacial lake.

I zipped up my coat all the way,
and stayed to watch
the geometric wonder.

Rhyming into the Sublime

I've been thinking about rhymed poems lately,
and this came to me this morning:
"The day is dark and dreary,
I feel so very weary."

But then it got stuck
in my mind like a looped tape.
I said, "No, stop it! The day is not dark and dreary."

I said, "Dammit, the day is sunny and funny."
Then I went on a walk with my honey.
Afterward, a new song came into my head,
but it wasn't mine.
It belonged to Johnny Nash.

I can see clearly now the rain is gone
I can see all obstacles in my way
Gone are the dark clouds that had me blind
It's gonna be a bright (bright)
Bright (bright) sunshiny day
It's gonna be a bright (bright)
Bright (bright) sunshiny day

*Lyrics from "I Can See Clearly Now" by Johnny Nash

The Gift

A box arrived on the front porch today,
and since I've just had a birthday,
I thought it might be a belated gift.

When I sliced it open, inside I spied a plastic bag marked
"Kramer."
I had forgotten we'd requested his ashes.
This was not the birthday gift I'd had in mind.

I teared up at this
final proof of his departure.
I miss him so much,
and thinking of him reminds me
what a treasure he was to our family.

It's not about the presents, it's
always about presence.

Once Every Seventeen Years

A whirring roar signals the onslaught
of their short existence.
I had forgotten this can last for six weeks.
It makes me want to stay indoors.

Husks cover our fence;
our dogs eat them.
Piles of dead cicadas fill
crevices at the bottom of our Oak trees.

One lone soldier, with eyes the color
of classic red nail polish,
emerges from the pyre,
ambling up the bark of the tree trunk.

They are everywhere.
Three cling
to a decorative crystal rock
in the garden as if its healing powers
could give them one more day.

Tiny burrows from where they burst forth
puncture the dirt throughout the flowerbeds.

The noise never stops-
a thousand maracas shaking all around me.

The Wisdom of Fifty-one

Fifty-one tells me I'm three decades to eighty-one.
Having worked in skilled care reminds me
that eighty-one can mean
your memory may slip like a heel on black ice,
you can't see it coming, but then one day
the bananas are in the pantry instead of the fruit bowl
and you don't know how that happened,
but you find peels bruising behind a box of Cheerios.

Or you might lose your words from having a stroke,
which also leaves half your mouth drooping,
so one side of your face looks like a comma;
the hand of your dead arm curls up into a fist
like a baby does when she cries.

You could end up in a nursing home for any variety of reasons,
and find yourself waiting for toileting assistance,
or worse, it's too late, and you need changing.

I once heard a woman shout,
"The only thing holding my poop in is my bones!"
And so, from where I'm sitting, these things make fifty-one look
pretty good.

Pause

Taking a moment
to sit in the sun and reflect.
How long has it been
since I've done this?

The move was horrendous,
but the worst of it is behind us.
I'm very happy to have
this moment, just to sit on our front stoop.

I'm looking out at the houses across the street.
So far, our new neighbors seem friendly.
This neighborhood is more eclectic, which suits me.

I notice there's no whir of cicadas.
They are dying off quickly now,
leaving eggs deeply in the ground,
a seventeen-year cycle starts anew.

Behind me, at our old house, is a decade
of raising tweens and teens to adulthood. All the tears-
both happy and sad ones, are gone.
I wonder what this cycle of living will bring.

My eyes are dry now, clearer,
and I'm free to replay the memories
of the past decade in my mind, if I choose.

Did I tell you I start a new job on Monday?

The sun gets too hot.
I rise to go inside,
looking up and ahead
 to what's next.

Colleen Wells is a journalist, poet, and memoirist. She is the author of the memoir, *Dinner with Doppelgangers—A True Story of Madness & Recovery* and *Animal Magnetism*, a poetry chapbook. Her work has appeared in several magazines and anthologies including *Adoptive Families Magazine, Chicken Soup for the Adoptive Soul, Gyroscope Review, NUVO, The Potomac Review, The RavensPerch* and the *Rockvale Review*.

Wells is a recipient of a 2023 Emerging Artist Grant awarded from the Bloomington Arts Commission, and a runner-up of the 2020 Robert Frost Award. She earned an Indiana Society of Professional Journalists Award - first place for feature writing in 2002.

Wells has facilitated poetry circles in nursing homes and helped preserve the wisdom of the elders in anthologies. As a guest writer at a local high school, she helped compile and edit students' mental illness narratives. She currently facilitates poetry circles for adults living with developmental disabilities.

Wells is a certified instructor for Journal to the Self, a journal keeping method created by Kathleen Adams, and completed TimeSlips story-telling training. She is in the process of becoming a Certified Therapeutic Recreation Specialist. Wells is active with the organization Women Writing for (a) Change Bloomington and helps with their outreach programming. She holds an M.F.A. from Spalding University. Wells currently works as a mental health professional and lives in Bloomington, IN.

www.ingramcontent.com/pod-product-compliance
Lightning Source LLC
Chambersburg PA
CBHW020219090426
42734CB00008B/1137